# Getting To One

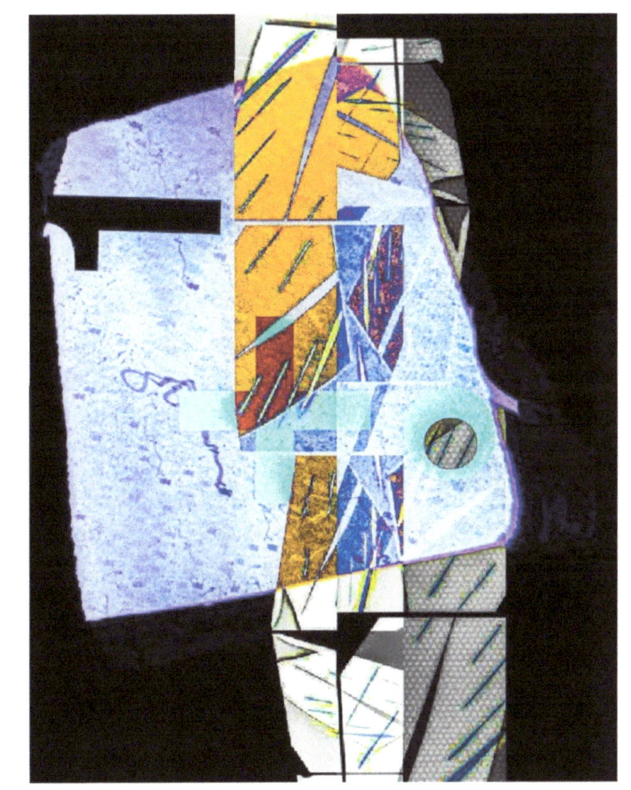

Flash Fictions by Eileen R. Tabios

Art by harry k stammer

Sandy Press

Cover design, cover preparation, & interior layout by

harry k stammer

ISBN: 978-1-7368160-7-3

"Planet M" was previously published in *Otoliths*, 2023, Editor Mark Young.

"One Eye Open," "Polmost Spirytus Rektyfikowany Vodka," "The Road to Juliana," and "Non-Fungible Armadillo Shells" were previously published in *The Brooklyn Rail*, 2023, Editor Anselm Berrigan.

"Ghost" was accepted for publication by Ravenna Press' "Triple Series," editor Kathryn Rantala

Printed in U.S.A.

**Sandy Press**

**Sandy-press.com**

## Contents

*After conceptualizing, then creating, "One"—a bar where each patron must drink alone—he became its most frequent patron.*

***—from "Ghost" by Eileen R. Tabios***

## The End Of Sundays

"I hope we'll be best friends when we grow up"—that's what he said to all of them. When he was young, his parents hosted children from the nearby orphanage for weekend visits. "To give them a break," his father said. He was happy to play with them and they seemed to reciprocate his joy. Instead of goodbyes, he would say at the end of Sundays, "I hope we'll be best friends when we grow up" because he knew there would be no return visits. His mother said, "There are so many orphans. Let's give everyone a turn." From those formative years, he grew to invent "One," a bar where each patron must drink alone. After hiring redhead bartenders and waiters because their hair was colored by passion, he became the bar's most frequent patron. One night, he looked up from his glass of Peacekeeper American Bourbon Whiskey that he'd bought for its bottle shaped like a mobile ICBM missile and, suddenly, all the other patrons felt familiar. His eyes traveled from one to another. His gaze rested on each long enough for them to feel its weight. They raised bowed heads to look back, fully revealing etched faces experienced with permanently delayed gratification. No one welcomed the recognition. Studies show that recognition boosts self-esteem, but that horse smashed down the paddock gate long ago before it galloped towards a lushly foliaged mountain on another continent. The other patrons were the best friends he'd longed for—a longing that introduced him to the hope that ended up hiding within the horse's green destination where azaleas, once likened to brooding and black coffee-drinking women, grew easily. How *easily* hope shrivels. Each had stepped unaccompanied into "One," and each would leave alone. Each departure marked the end of a Sunday.

r said. Fro
ne,” a bar
rtender an
he nig
all the othe

## Planet M

Turn left and you're on your knees. You're raising your right hand to a long-haired lady, a platinum ring topped by a 3-karat diamond pinched by your trembling fingers. She's widening her eyes to drink in your marriage proposal. You both will live happily ever after. Turn right and you're tripping over the hem of your monk's robe. You catch yourself and continue striding into the dim entrance of a stone building. You exit into the monastery's interior courtyard where the light is blinding as its walls bask under a noonday sun. These situations—and many others—are offered by the glass walls bordering the paths through which you navigate this planet. Your own body is not involved, just the avatars presented by mirrors. Your race has depended on video screens and selfies for so long that none of this is unusual. What is unusual is when you trip non-virtually and smash your face against a mirrored wall. You are shocked when you feel your brow sunder and the escaping blood paints the walls around you. You raise a hand to feel the warmth of ichor though your veins are not a god's. You look at your bloodied hand and notice how it's become the same color as the smears on the cracked mirror facing you. For the first time, you notice Planet M, the world of mirrors that's evolved around you. You notice how this planet lacks aroma. Perfume has become extinct—once upon a time, you'd favored a lover's scent of refined citrus accord and geranium as exalted sensually by smooth woods, bourbon, dark patchouli, black amber and cashmere musk while emitting subtle notes of orange, ruby red grapefruit, Mandarin, geranium, bourbon, and dark patchouli—but you don't know how to weep at the disappearance of fragrance. You don't know how to mourn evaporation. You only know you created Planet M from sitting too long at the counter of "One," a bar where each patron must drink alone.

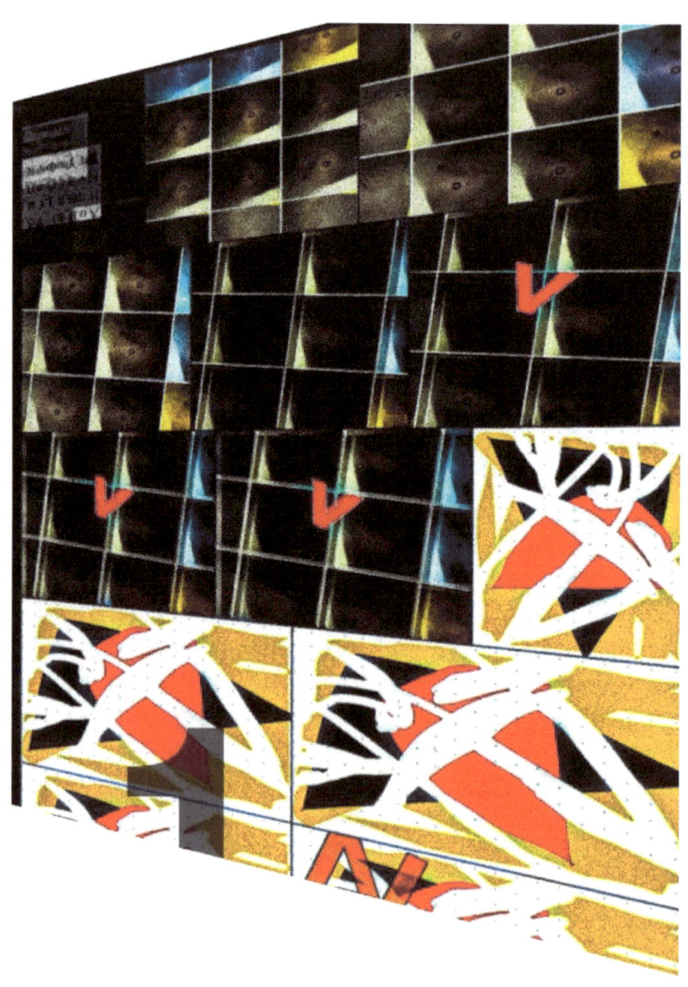

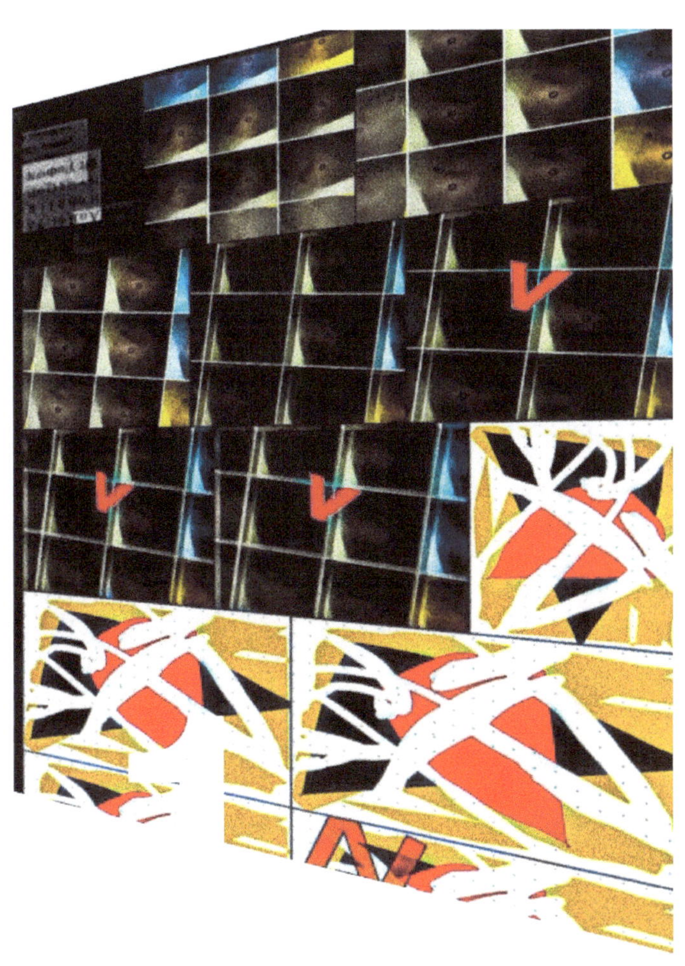

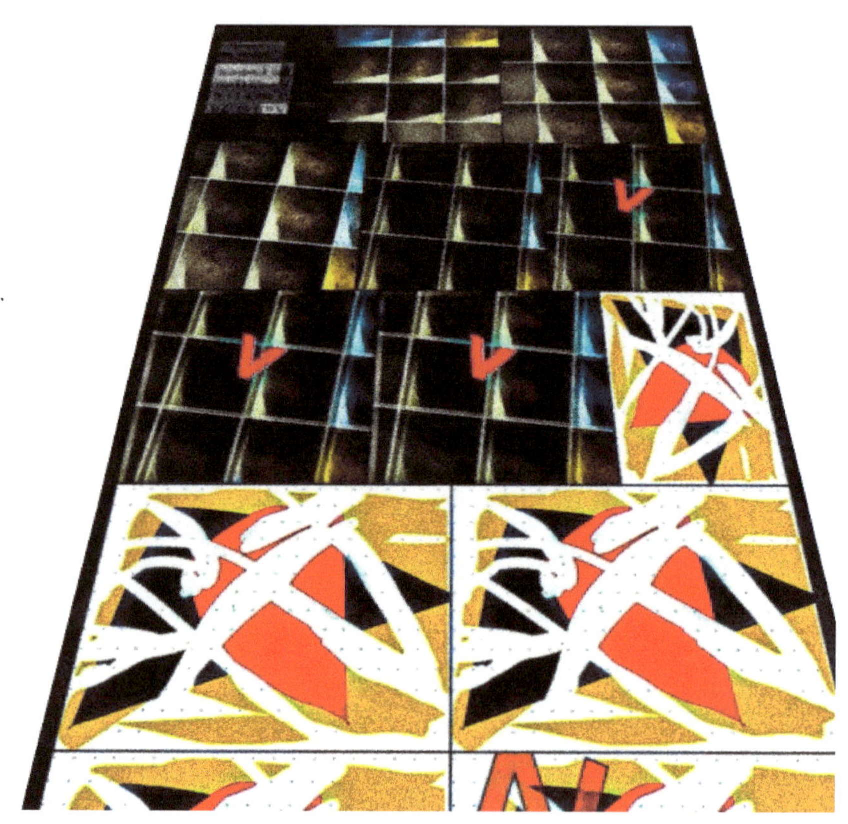

## Polmost Spirytus Rektyfikowany Vodka

He woke from a dream of Chichen Itza where he'd followed the serpent descending the step pyramid of the Kukulcan temple. When he left its last step, he stumbled out of the dream to feel his cheek hardening against a wood counter. He raised his head to see the bartender looking at him quizzically as she raised a bottle of Polmost Spirytus Rektyfikowany Vodka. "You sure?" the bartender asked, flinging back wavy red hair over gleaming white shoulders bared by a strapless top. The vodka was the world's strongest alcoholic drink, courtesy of Poland. At 192 proof, it was banned from even checked baggage traveling into the United States. He'd excavated it in New Zealand from a wine cellar owned by a Silicon Valley financier who built an escapist utopia on the island country. He'd filed one of the cases in the bar for his private stash. "Not sure. But pour it anyway," he replied. As she filled the glass before him, he asked, "Do you know the word 'seasteading'?" "Nope." "It means creating artificial islands." He'd learned the term after punishing the financier for hiring mercenaries to assassinate a Māori activist concerned about the safety of sea creatures. The bartender snorted. "If folks want to live on islands, they should just come here." He nodded and tried to recall his dream—he was searching Chichen Itza for a mural depicting the Mayan rain god Cháak. The mural featured Maya Blue, a color he needed to see to verify he'd successfully recreated the technique for making it. He'd found the dye's source in the Ch'oj plant growing in Quintana Roo. But he'd had to persevere through tests that initially disputed its existence. A cloth soaked in its dye first turned white; only prolonged immersion turned it blue. "I was unnerved by that white smoke until the vibrant turquoise broke through," he explained to the bartender. "No one ever talks about how much fortitude hope requires." The redhead looked at him closely. "But you didn't lose hope," she said. "So what are you doing *here*?" He looked around. He laughed. He was in "One," a bar where each patron must enter alone, drink alone, and leave alone. He laughed again as he waved at her to refill his glass. "A toast to Polmost," he said with a grin. "It made me forget I both lack hope and am hopeless."

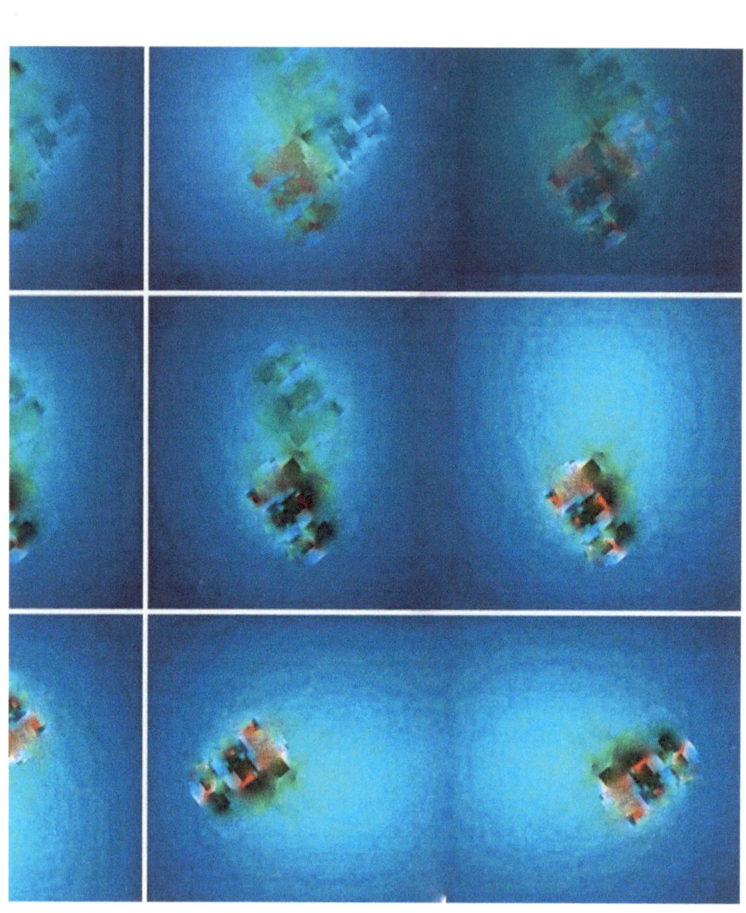

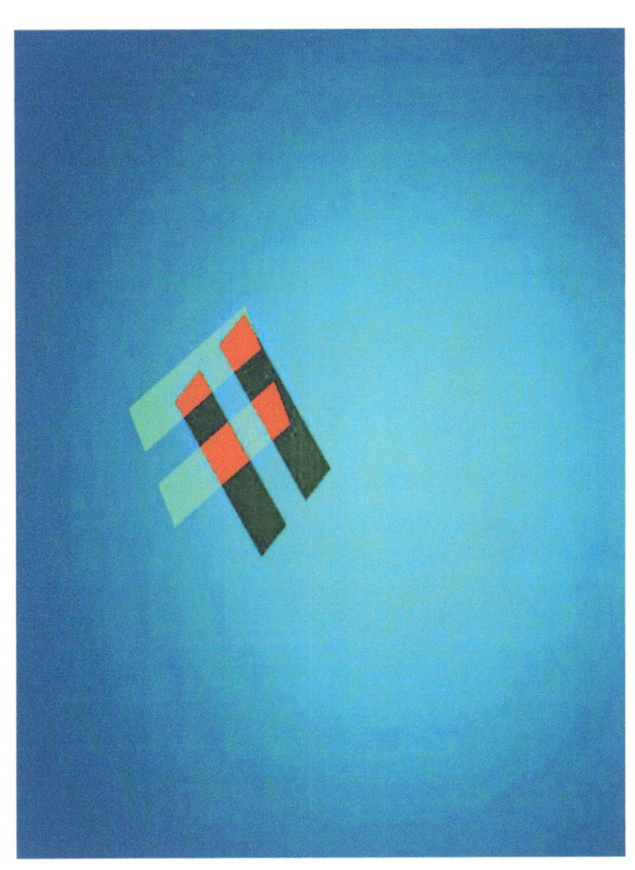

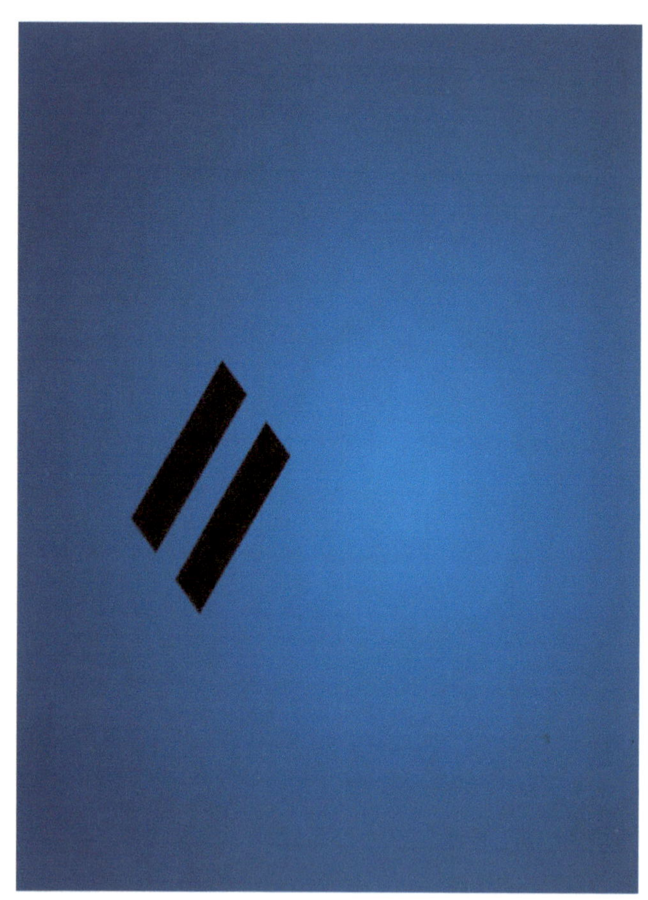

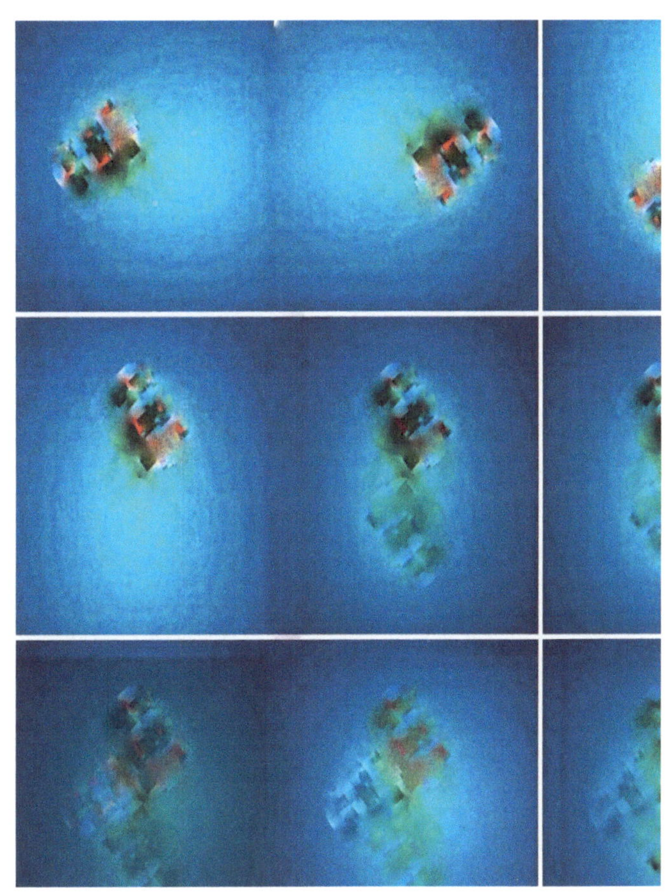

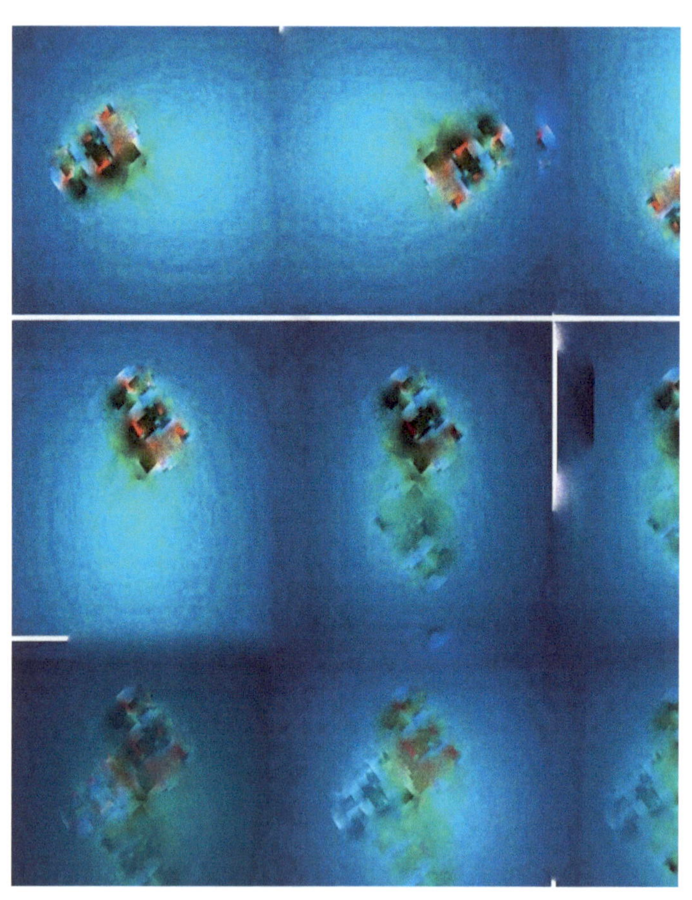

## Ghost

Legendary CIA spy Krii Amman once swayed atop a table in Ye Olde Cheshire Cheese, the London pub known for its regulars Mark Twain, Sir Arthur Conan Doyle, and a foul-mouthed parrot called Polly who spewed profanities and entertained drinkers by imitating a cork popping followed by the glug, glug, glug of wine being poured. (Stuffed after his death, Polly remains in a cage above the bar.) Krii regaled the equally drunk denizens of the night with a rendition of "Invictus," the poem inspired by William Ernest Henley's homage to strength in the face of adversity, in his case, the tuberculosis that threatened to amputate his remaining leg. The Victorian poet had traveled to Edinburgh where the distinguished surgeon Joseph Lister saved his leg. While recovering in the infirmary, he wrote the verses that became "Invictus," an evocation of stoicism or the British "stiff upper lip."

> Out of the night that covers me
> Black as the pit from pole to pole,
> I thank whatever gods may be
> For my unconquerable soul.
>
> In the fell clutch of circumstance,
> I have not winced nor cried aloud.
> Under the bludgeonings of chance
> My head is bloody, but unbowed.

Etcetera etcetera. Though drunk, many in the crowd—perhaps remembering their youthful schooling—recollected the poem's last two lines to shout with Krii the poem's resounding conclusion:

> *I am the master of my fate!*
> *I am the captain of my soul!*

One of the boozy yellers was so charmed that he invited Krii home to sleep off the Imperial Stouts. The pub had just thrown everyone out for the morning janitor to do his mopping. Hands across each other's shoulders, Krii and his new best friend entered with their stench through the front door opened by Krii's target, his friend's father, Liam Ebersold. Not only did Mr. Ebersold spawn an alcoholic but he'd also instigated what the CIA called the "Covid

Scattergun." Mr. Ebersold masterminded an attempt to infiltrate the U.S. with Covid-infected drug addicts sourced from his share of the illegal drug trade. San Diego was nearly annihilated before the CIA and other authorities shut down his portion of the hundred trillion-dollar activity that comprised 1% of total global trade. The United States took its revenge with Krii's invasion of the Ebersold household. Once inside a foyer ironically decorated with lovely floral wallpaper, Krii turned the son unconscious with a rear naked choke before dispatching two bullets into the father's brain. Recalling a line once pronounced by poet Andrew Joron, he whispered, "Flowers can be ferocious" at Gucci's English rose wallpaper produced on green and pink linen by Italian artisans.

But Krii never anticipated that a career stuffed with such moments would bring him to "One," a bar where each patron must drink alone. Krii did not anticipate that each killing would also kill a part of himself. At "One," he could camouflage how he'd turned himself into a ghost.

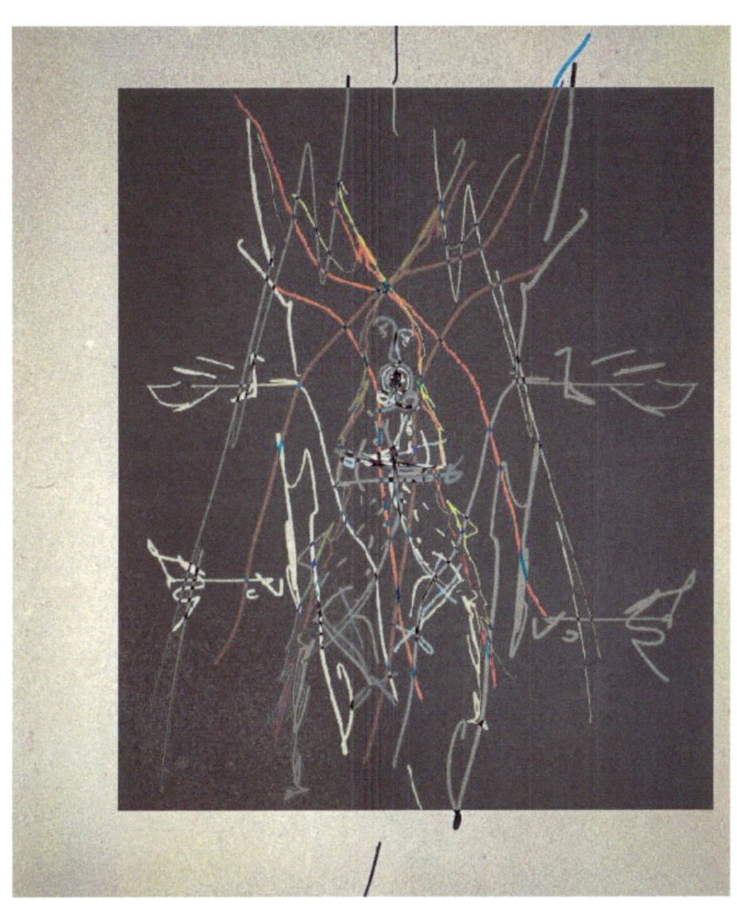

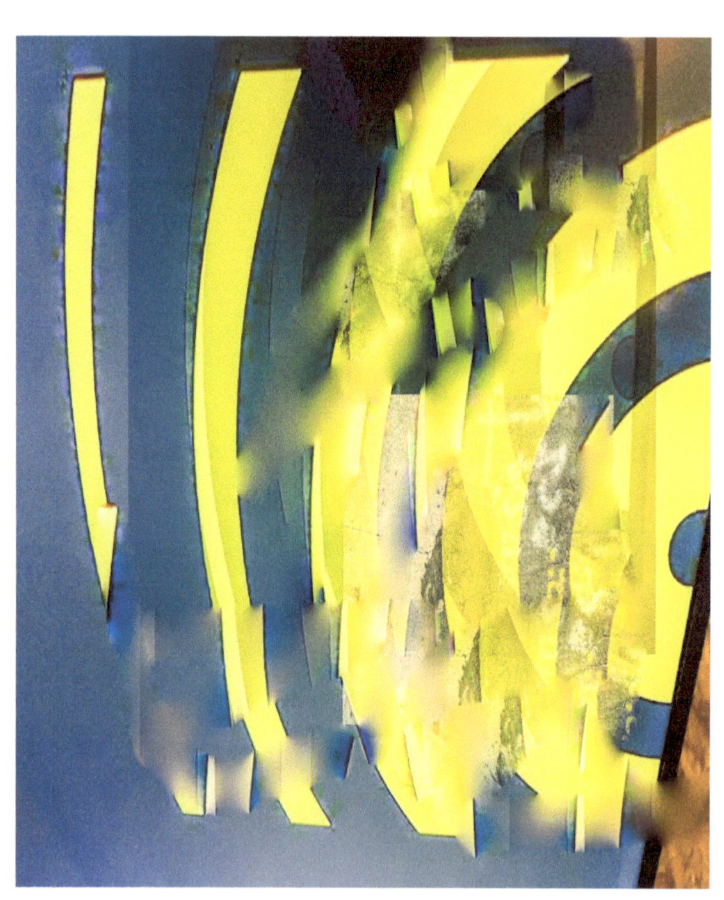

## The Road to Juliana

He wasn't sleepy but yawned to regulate his body temperature—that was his token health activity. Nor did he use the yawn for briefly closing his eyes—he was cognizant the eye's cornea is the only body part without a blood supply, getting its oxygen directly from air. Logically, his glass contained tequila which, according to mice studies, may be best for blood sugar balance among alcoholic beverages due to the naturally occurring sugar in its base of the agave plant. Other studies conclude tequila may not be as severe a depressant as other types of alcohol. He wondered whether he'd drink as much tequila as the amount of saliva a human produces in a lifetime, a volume sufficient to fill two swimming pools. These are the concerns of a former dietitian before becoming a regular at "One," a bar where each patron must drink alone. He looked forward to forgetting his past—at least his thoughts will come to lessen their concern over health which was no longer relevant for his life. His past reveals him as a victim of how the field of eating disorders presents a high burn out rate for dietitians who constantly take in their clients' anxiety and trauma. *Fuhgetaboutit!* he thought. *Learn about dogs,* he ordered himself. *Dogs benefit humans!* This was how he discovered that a Great Dane named Juliana once peed on an incendiary bomb during World War II, thereby earning a Blue Cross Medal.

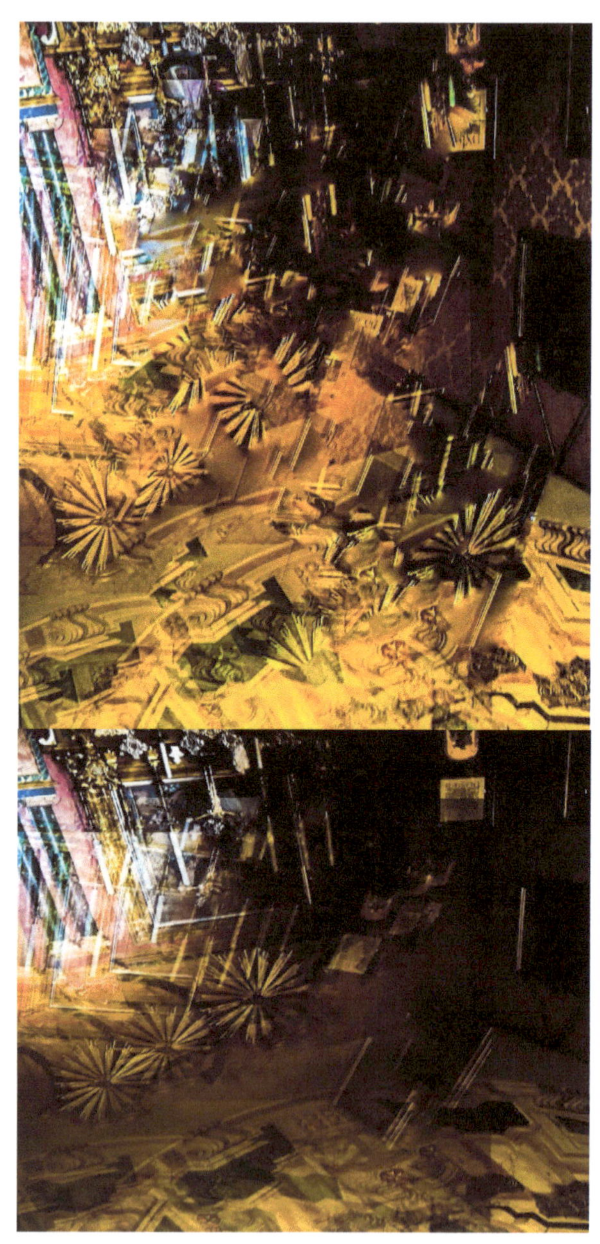

## One Eye Open

He sometimes wondered if he should wear an eye-patch to mask how his left eye hid under its constantly lowered eyelid. But he couldn't release dolphins from his memory and chose to be transparent about his shuttered eye. Before retirement, he'd worked for a company that turned dead bodies into ocean reefs—the company named itself "Eternal Reefs." Trawling oceanic depths, he stumbled across a pod of dolphins. He smiled at them, manifesting the long ties between their species. The ancient Greeks and their gods welcomed dolphins—emblazoned on their coins, they were sacred to both Aphrodite and Apollo. In Hindu mythology, the Ganges river dolphin is associated with Ganga, the deity of the Ganges river. The Boto, a species of river dolphin that resides in the Amazon River, are believed to be shapeshifters, or *encantados*, capable of bearing children with humans. On land, studying them, he stumbled across research revealing how dolphins are sufficiently intelligent to be capable of self-awareness, the precursor to advanced thought processes like meta-cognitive reasoning (thinking about thinking) attributed to humans. Events that blackened sky before nighttime then transpired to interrupt his meditations on dolphins. Those events explained the logic to how dolphins sleep—with one eye open. Those events continued so that he, too, began sleeping with one eye open. Eventually, the only source of succor left to him was "One," a bar where patrons must drink alone. He felt relief at being in a place where no one was allowed to bother him. But he'd seen how the affable dolphin sleeps, and so drank his bourbon with one eye open. Paradoxically, one open eye made him more watchful than two open eyes. Blindness, even in one eye, emphasizes one's fragility through exposure to events that randomly create collateral damage, whether from humans who are the planet's most dangerous species or panda cubs smaller than mice and each weighing no more than four ounces. To look at a panda cub is to feel one's heart constrict from the ineffable so that, helplessly, tears begin to leak.

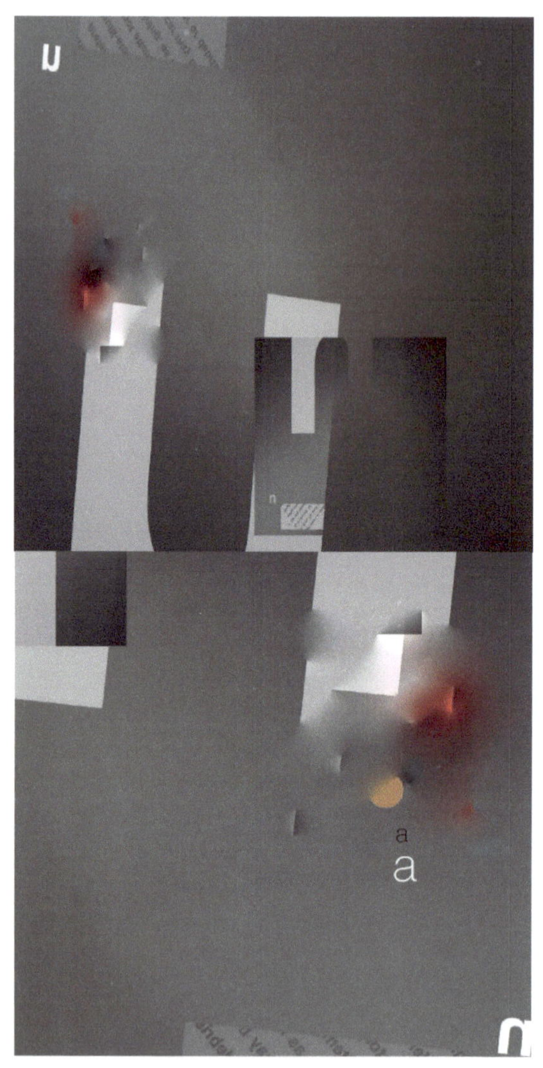

## "Spies Favor Red Velvet Cupcakes"

Like the others, he rarely spoke beyond ordering the first fill and subsequent refills—such was the usual state of play at "One," a bar where individual patrons must drink alone. But, this time, he drank too much, and no one could stop him from droning non-stop for an hour. The first time a waiter cautioned him, he yelled, "I am Walsingham's descendant!" Then he continued rambling. On their way to the bathroom, lingering passersby could discern his monologue's theme: "characteristics of spies." Like,

> Never forget the spy who died because she applied the term "champagne" to California sparkling wine—her mistake revealed her as an impostor to the Russian oenophile who trafficked in top-shelf prostitutes. Offended, the foodie oligarch recalled the basil on his beloved dish of *insalata caprese*, and chiffonaded her head in one of his 10,000-bottle wine cellars sprinkled around the planet. Spies must do their homework well, if only to avoid having their heads sliced into thin strips.
>
> Flexibility. Or as known in the U.S. military, "Semper Gumby," dog Latin for "Always Flexible." The motto is a play on "Semper Fidelis" (U.S. Marine Corp motto that means "Always Faithful") and "Semper fortis" (U.S. Coast Guard motto that means "Always Strong"). Gumby was an American green clay character whose name replaced the second word of what would be the flexibility motto in true Latin: "Semper Flexibilis."
>
> That spies live on the spectrum of sociopathy. Nor do they mind… much. Because they share a certain knowledge with surgeons: a wound can be erased by creating a deeper wound from which fresh skin arises to fill the aftermath of what was sundered during battle.
>
> Affability—it can be helpful in a spy's weaponry. Like honey, affability can mire, attract, or fool the enemy. It is more insidious than fear.

The paradox of spies avoiding crying when tears improve sight.

Spies favor red velvet cupcakes because said cupcakes symbolize the opposites of their lives.

Spies don't trust endorphins.

Finally, the redhead came out from behind the bar and raised the blathering man by his armpits, dragged him to the exit, and threw him out onto the asphalt road gleaming under the newly departed rain like Einstein's brow when his brain overheated. The bartender thought, *Huzzah for the 3Pees!* "3Pees" referred to her favored strength-training exercises: push-ups, pull-ups, and planks. As the garrulous spymaster fell, a waiter who followed them yelled: "Here's one: spies don't admire rainbows because they smash them!"

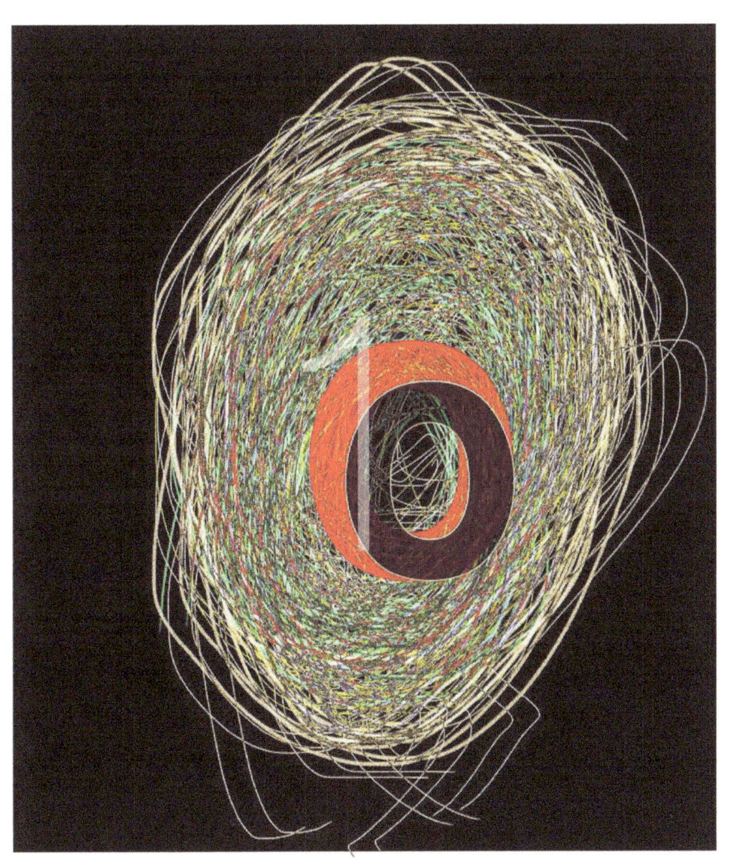

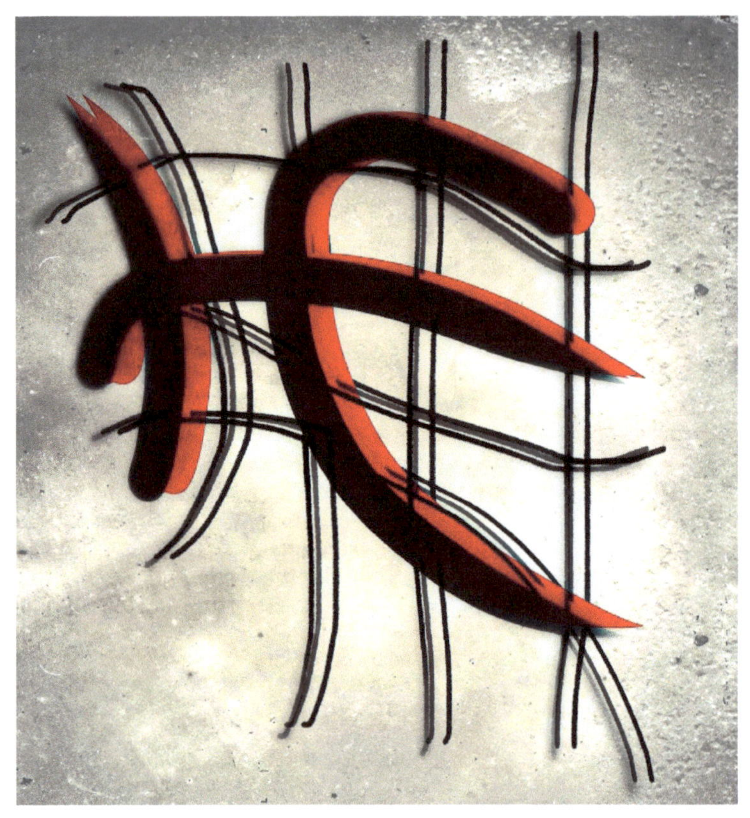

## Silence as Condition Precedent

His stomach growled since he refused to do as the Koreans do when they drink their soju. The bartender heard and offered him a bowl of miniature pretzels and Wasabi-infused nuts. He waved away the bowl but she pushed it closer to him. She swiped red bangs away from her eyes as she said, "I don't like ghosts and anything related to ghosts. When your stomach growls, I'm reminded of ghost crabs who literally growl by using the teeth in their stomachs." He emptied his glass and waved it back and forth for a refill. "Don't turn me into a honeybee waving my glass as rapidly as honeybees flap their wings 230 times every second." Her bangs fell again as he spoke and she blew them away from her stare to reply, "You're drinking too much. You're not like the Turritopsis dohrnii, those eternal jellyfish that, in response to physical damage, revert in their development process to a polyp." When he couldn't come up with another esoteric animal fact, she leaned closer for the proverbial kill. "Snails can sleep up to three years if the weather isn't moist enough to meet their needs." Shuddering, he drew back from her gaze and backed away from the counter. After a few feet, he turned and limped towards the exit. A waiter approached the redhead. As they watched him push open the door and leave, he whispered, "It's amazing how you learned his language just so you can order him to leave. What'd he do to irritate you?" She scowled. "He's a pretender. He claims to prefer being alone but he needs company to listen to his animal stories." The waiter nodded, then left to take another customer's order. At "One," a bar where patrons can only drink alone, drunks became regulars only if they'd lost all appetite to be heard.

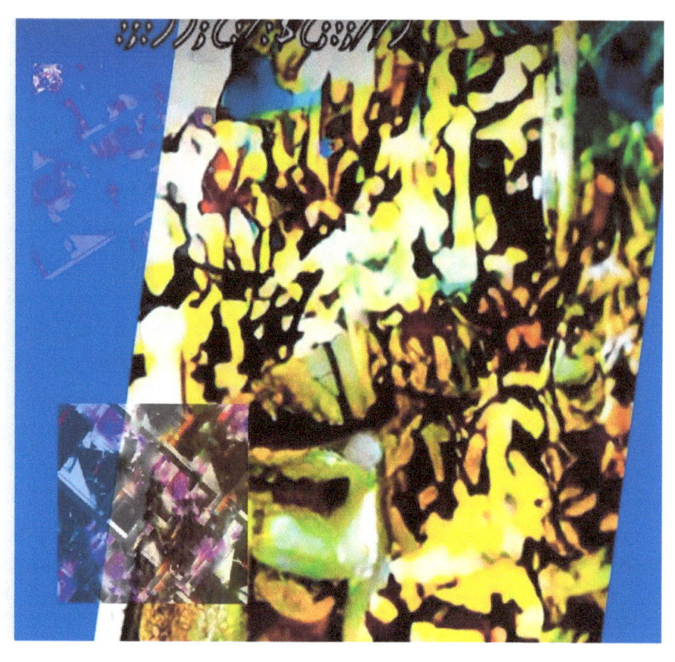

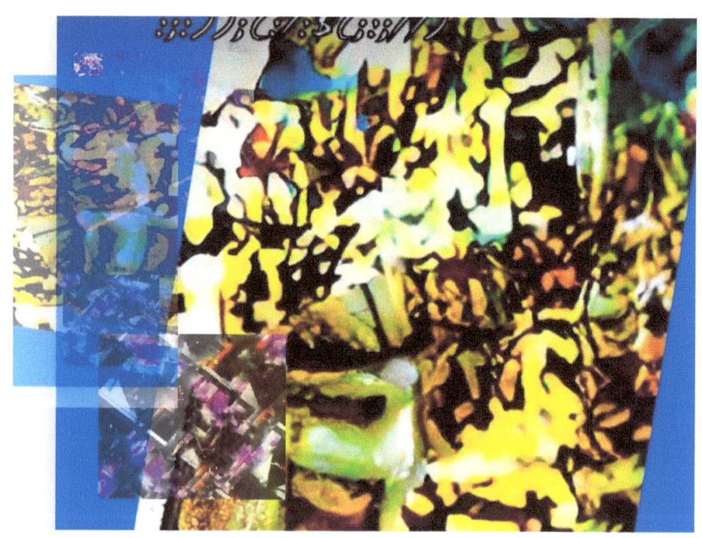

## Brutality

Mr. Doe felt the ghost of Lord Elgin on the empty chair across the table. Britain's Ambassador in Constantinople at the start of the 19$^{th}$ century, had stripped the Parthenon of its most beautiful marbles, over 200 blocks now ensconced in the British Museum. While interest has focused on the stolen marbles, less attention has been paid to how Lord Elgin came to visit the Parthenon: through a royal decree by the Great Vizir authorizing him to do sketches and castings of the Parthenon and its friezes. A century-and-a-half later, the sketches were scheduled to be exhibited at the Bogota Museum of Paper, which was how Mr. Doe came to steal the sketches; he planned to keep them within his private collection until the British returned all Parthenon marbles to Greece.

Mr. Doe hired Laura of Clan 18, one of Bogota's gangs, to hijack the sketches during their transport from the airport to the museum. Laura decided to seduce the manager of its transfer, Gordo. She became his girlfriend some weeks before the scheduled theft. Gordo was exactly what his nickname stated: fat, correction, *huge* at nearly 7 feet tall and 450 pounds. Such girth, while impressive, made him unpalatable to most ladies in the market for a romantic relationship. Since Laura was a natural beauty and even more charismatic when she shoved her cleavage high through push-up bras, Gordo fell... heavily.

She stroked Gordo's ego by professing awe at his importance for being charged with abducting Lord Elgin's sketches, which was how she convinced Gordo it was his idea to bring her along for the ride. To make a long story short, Laura, an expert in the Soviet martial arts of combat sambo, overcame Gordo and brought their car to a location where three ruthless members of her gang waited. They then scooted off with the sketches they later traded for beaucoo bucks with Mr. Doe. During the hand-off, more to make nervous conversation with the bad-ass-looking gang members than curiosity, Mr. Doe asked, "What happened to Gordo?"

Laura paused, then traded glances with the others. None could hold it in for long: they started laughing, with one actually falling to the ground as he held on to his belly. "How to put this?" Laura began, before succumbing to more laughter. One of the ruthless ones finally explained—'twas easy enough to put several bullets into Gordo's big head. But then they field dressed Gordo as if he was a moose. Yes, a moose. Apparently, they'd trained themselves through YouTube videos of Alaskan hunters field-dressing huge animals. They cut up Gordo's remains and wrapped his meat portions in butcher paper. Later, they offloaded Gordo as beef to a restaurant due to host the engagement party of a rival gang's leader.

Mr. Doe had sold the sketches long ago to another collector. He could not abide the memories that accompanied them—a big man being field-dressed into generous slabs of faux filet mignons. This is how, unbeknownst to the staff of "One," a bar where each patron must drink alone, he always has company as he downs shot glasses of the bar's oldest whisky. The whiskey boasts a dark amber color as well as a nose of cinnamon and gingerbread with hints of orange and oak. The palate opens brightly with orange notes before giving way to cinnamon, clove, and gingerbread, followed by a long, spicy finish. Across Mr. Doe's table, Lord Elgin drank as if ghosts were solid and could drink. Lord Elgin even waxed enthusiastically over how the whiskey was made: "It begins with a 100% corn mash bill aged three years in a heavily charred Virginia red wine barrel. The spirit's then transferred into a charred Cinnamon Whiskey barrel where it ages for a year. Then it's transferred again into a used #4 char bourbon barrel where it rests for an additional year, culminating in a one-of-a-kind 5-year-aged whiskey!"

Then Lord Elgin would burp and conclude as he always did with the whisky's name, his wet tongue caressing each syllable: "Bru-tal-i-ty! *Brutality!*"

Sipping at his cruel drink, Mr. Doe would nod in miserable agreement. "Brutality."

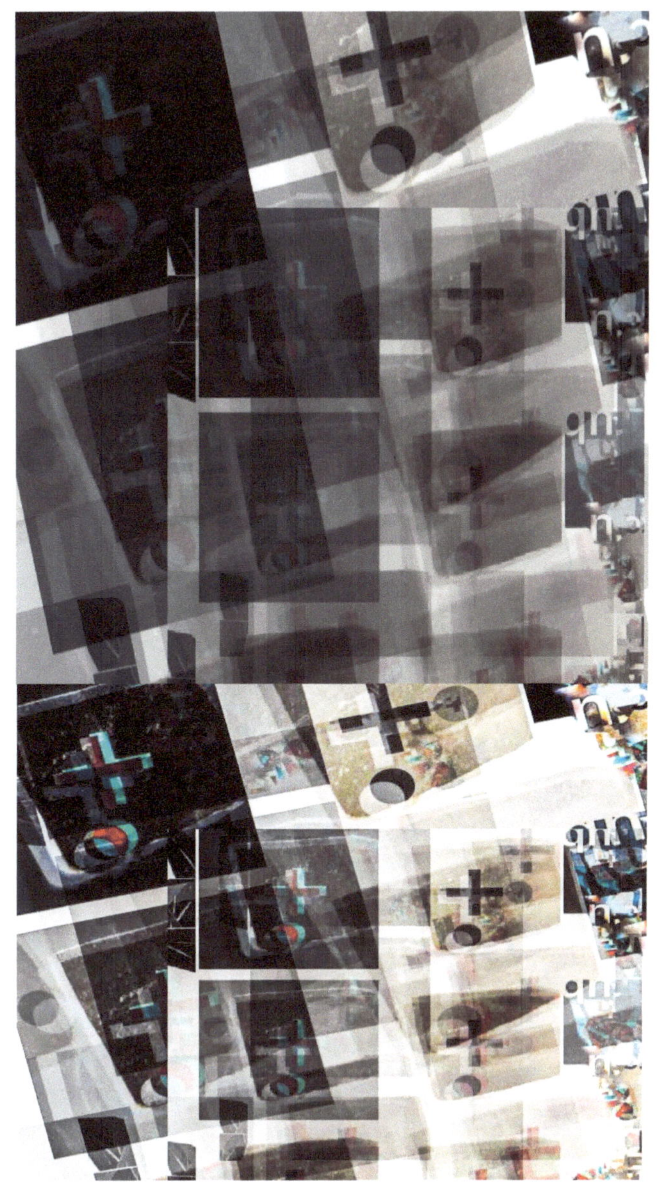

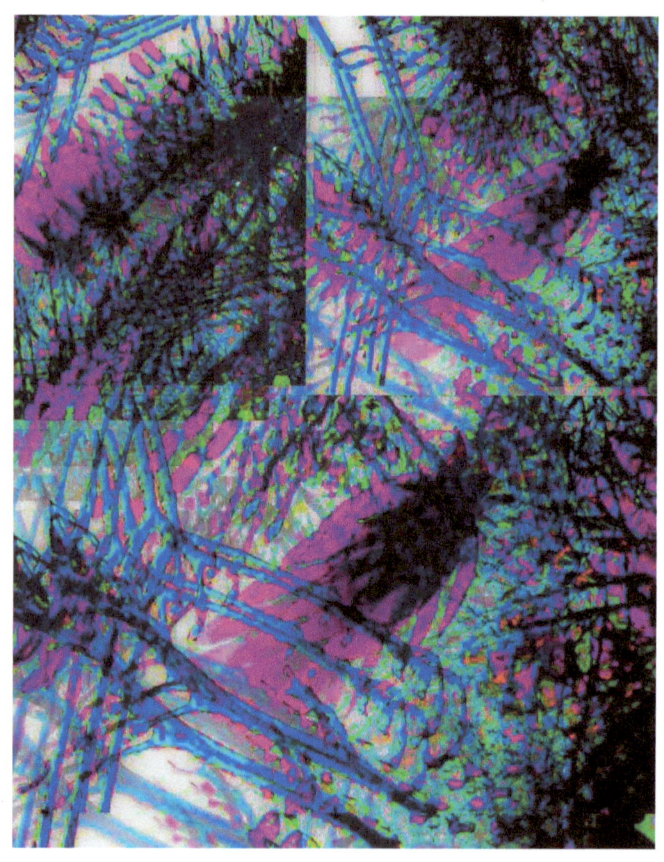

## Non-Fungible Armadillo Shells

Soon, the waiters noticed how the man's lips only stopped moving when he sipped from his glass of Reyka vodka. Nearby, the television's Talking Heads debated whether NFTs could work as Pokemon cards, a discussion that involved the bored apes owned by Jimmy Fallon and Paris Hilton as well as how Beeple's NFT collage, *Everydays: The first 5000 Days*, sold at Christie's for $69 million, about $15 million more than what Monet's *Nymphéas* sold for in 2014. One waiter approached the muttering man. But the man's muttering was too low for the waiter to hear clearly. So he moved closer to the experienced drunk and observed, "Reyka is a uniquely Icelandic splash in the vodka world. The distiller makes its spirit from a glacier's pure spring water after the water passes through a 4,000-year-old lava field." The man turned his face towards the waiter who took a step back at seeing eyes not just blood-red but with blood leaking from its sides. "TV people are idiots," the man whispered. "I turned a boy into a paraplegic because it's impossible to turn an armadillo into an NFT." Such was how the waiters at "One," a bar where each patron must drink alone, came to pity the man with red eyes whose mutterings were simply a repetition of the one word, "idiot." Unlike many on the planet, armadillo shells are bulletproof. Outside the bar, the crumpled receipt for an NFT that failed to shield a boy manifests *flotsam and jetsam* as it keeps being picked up by a harsh wind that blows it down dim and smelly alleys leading nowhere.

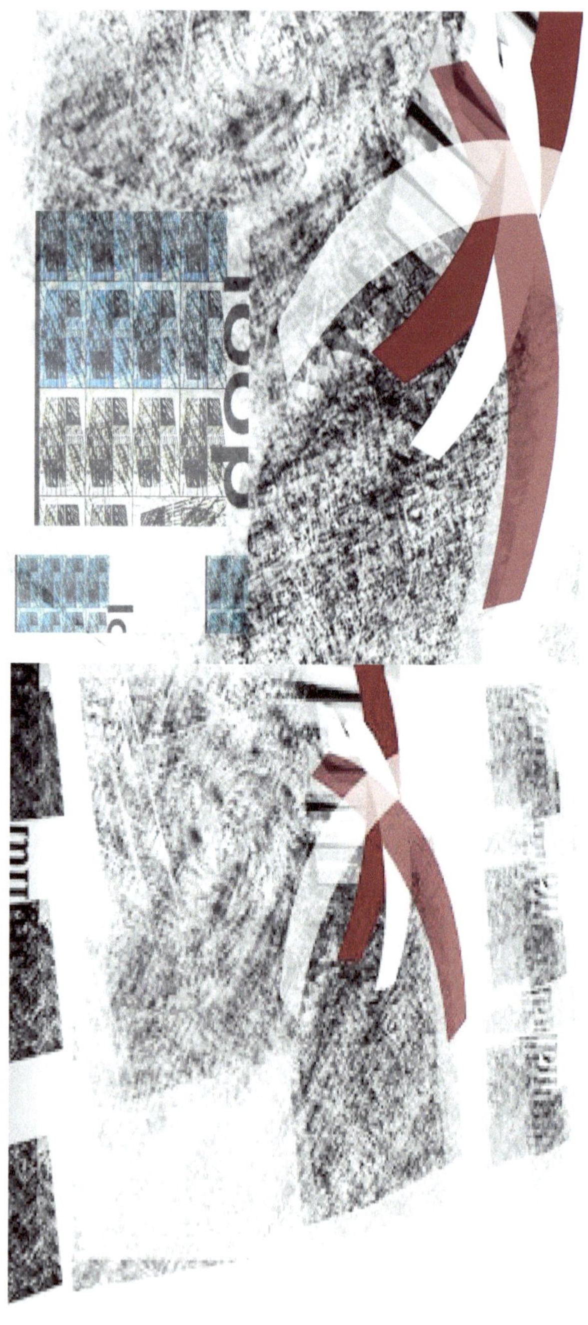

## Guilty Pleasure Music

wafted from speakers behind the bar. The only one who showed a reaction was the fellow with a man-bun whose lips started singing along without sound. The Hindley Street Country Club, featuring Glenn Cunningham, was covering "Biggest Part of Me" by Ambrosia. The love song almost made many patrons forget why they ended up at "One," a bar where each patron must drink alone. But their memories returned before the end of any song that might temporarily transport them elsewhere—as if one never spent years living as a stowaway on cargo trains, as if one didn't spend two decades hunting serial killers, as if one was never sold by a drug addict mother, as if one didn't escape from Mariupol where he'd joined conscripted Russians ordered to scrub the city of its Ukrainian identity by renaming street names with Soviet ones and enforcing a Russian curriculum within its schools. Other stories tangoed with a wide variety of alcohol among the patrons—tales that refused the succor of or erasure by pleasurable music. At "One," pleasure was a source of guilt and not something to be shared—it was better to remain at one with one's self.

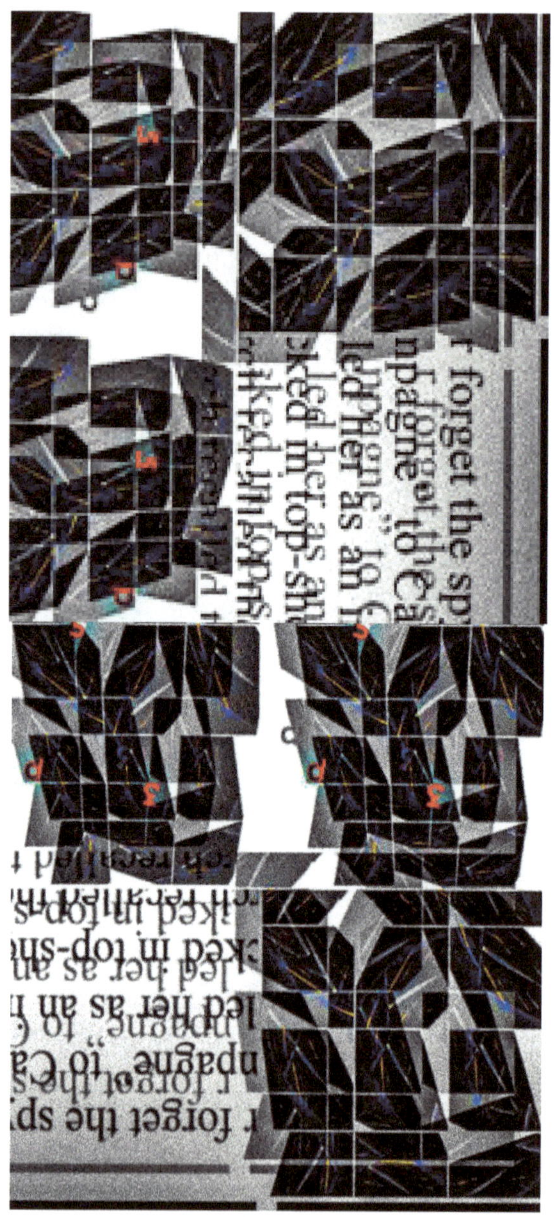

## Recyled Afterthought

One night, you looked up from your glass of Peacekeeper American Bourbon Whiskey that you'd bought for its bottle shaped like a mobile ICBM missile and, suddenly, all the other patrons felt familiar. Perfume was extinct—once upon a time, you'd favored a lover's scent of refined citrus accord and geranium as exalted sensually by smooth woods, bourbon, dark patchouli, black amber, and cashmere musk while emitting subtle notes of orange, ruby red grapefruit, Mandarin, geranium, bourbon, and dark patchouli—but you don't know how to weep at the disappearance of fragrance. You were in "One," a bar where each patron must enter alone, drink alone, and leave alone. Recalling a line once pronounced by poet Andrew Joron, you whispered, "Flowers can be ferocious" at Gucci's English rose wallpaper produced on green and pink linen by Italian artisans. You wondered whether you'll drink as much tequila as the amount of saliva a human produces in a lifetime—a volume sufficient to fill two swimming pools. You felt relief at being in a place where no one was allowed to bother you. Because spies share a certain knowledge with surgeons: a wound can be erased by creating a deeper wound from which fresh skin arises to fill the aftermath of what was sundered during battle. Your stomach growled since you refused to do as the Koreans do when they drink their soju. You could not abide the memory of a big man being field-dressed into generous slabs of faux filet mignons. Nearby, the television's Talking Heads debated whether NFTs could work as Pokemon cards, a discussion that involved the bored apes owned by Jimmy Fallon and Paris Hilton as well as how Beeple's NFT collage, *Everydays: The first 5000 Days*, sold at Christie's for $69 million, about $15 million more than what Monet's *Nymphéas* sold for in 2014. At "One," pleasure was a source of guilt and not something to be shared—it was better to remain at one with one's self.

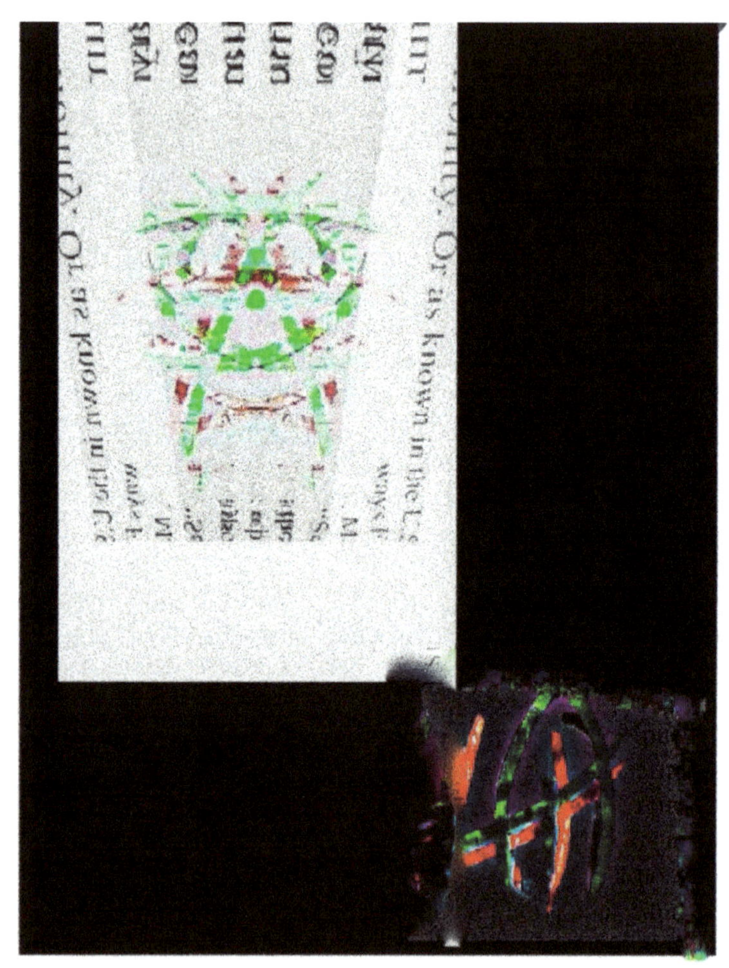
Or as known in the

## Process Note: Art

The artwork for *Getting To One* was created as a group of non-representational pieces that allow the reader to go further into the thoughts and emotions of the written work. All the artwork reflects on the whole and the parts equally by using a vispo approach with the number "1" and the word "one" as seeds to draw the two together. The reader is invited to make a connection between the text and the artwork.

—harry k stammer

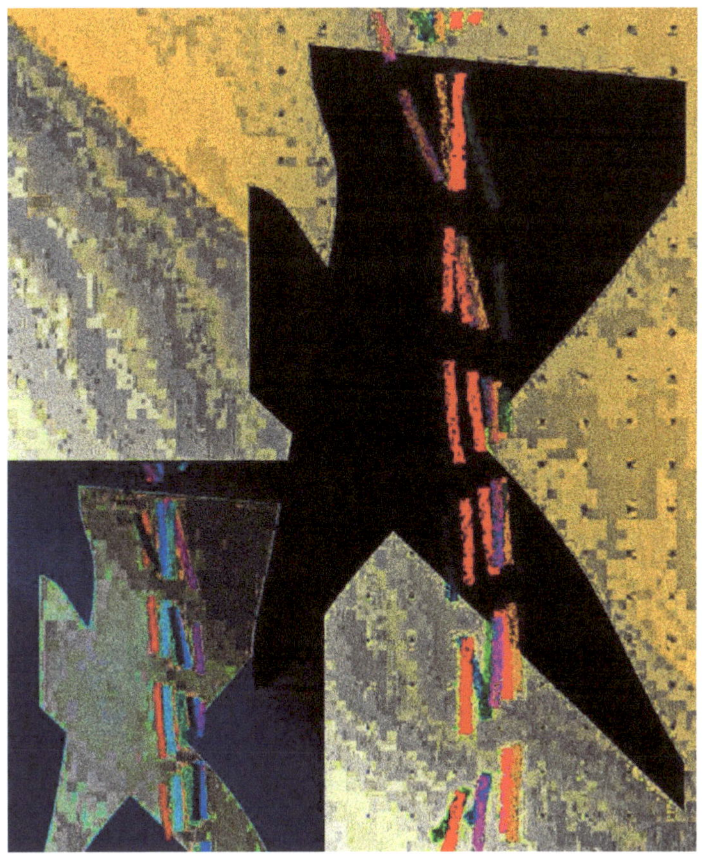

## Selected Notes & Bibliography to Flash Fictions

### The End of Sundays

"Why Recognition Is So Important (Top 7 Reasons)" by Matt Tenney, *Business Leadership Today*. https://businessleadershiptoday.com/why-is-recognition-so-important/

"The Peacekeeper American Bourbon Whiskey, Rancho Liquor. https://rancholiquoronline.com/the-peacekeeper-american-bourbon-whiskey/

"Minuteman Missile," MinuteManMissile.com. https://minutemanmissile.com/sicbm.html

"Hardest Flowers to Grow and Maintain," *Fresh Trimmings*. https://bouqs.com/blog/hardest-flowers-to-grow/

### Planet M

Perfume notes from *VOLUPTUOUS Eau de Parfum*

### Polmost Spirytus Rektyfikowany Vodka

"Artist rediscovers mysterious recipe for ancient 'Maya Blue' dye" by Mark Viales, *Mexico News Daily*, March 14, 2023

### Ghost

This is a reworked excerpt from Eileen R. Tabios' novel-in-progress, *Clandestine DNA*.

### The Road to Juliana

"50+ Weird but True Facts That Will Blow Your Mind" by Julie Sprankles, *Scary Mommy*, April 29, 2021

"8 Alcohols That Have Health Perks & How to Enjoy Them Mindfully" by Jessica Timmons, *mbgfood*, Nov. 2, 2022

"Top 10 Common Mistakes I Made as a New Dietitian: Part 1" by Jessi Kilbarger, *lknutrition*, March 6, 2022

### One Eye Open

"50+ Weird but True Facts That Will Blow Your Mind" by Julie Sprankles, *Scary Mommy*, April 29, 2021

Wikipedia on dolphins

**"Spies Favor Red Velvet Cupcakes"**

This combines excerpts from Eileen R. Tabios' novel-in-progress, *Clandestine DNA.*

Merriam-Webster on defining "spymaster". https://www.merriam-webster.com/dictionary/spymaster

"The 10 Best Strength-Training Exercises to Feel Strong and Confident" by Julie Floyd Jones, *EatingWell*, Feb. 28, 2022. https://www.eatingwell.com/article/7949443/best-strength-training-exercises/

**Silence as Condition Precedent**

"50+ Weird but True Facts That Will Blow Your Mind" by Julie Sprankles, *Scary Mommy*, April 29, 2021

**Brutality**

This is a reworked excerpt from Eileen R. Tabios' novel-in-progress, *Clandestine DNA.*

"Brutality," MurLarkey, nd

"Top 10 Deadliest Martial Arts in the World," *Lines*, nd

**Non-Fungible Armadillo Shells**

"NFTs, explained" by Mitchell Clark, *The Verge*, June 6, 2022

"Beeple sold an NFT for $69 million" by Jacob Kastrenakes, *The Verge*, March 11, 2021

"Top 15 Cheap Vodka Brands That Won't Break the Bank" by Paul Kushner, *My Bartender*, February 2023

***Guilty Pleasure Music***

"Russia scrubs Mariupol's Ukraine identity, builds on death" by Lori Hinnant, Vasilisa Stepanenko, Sarah El Deeb and Elizaveta Tilna, *Associated Press*, Dec. 22, 2002

**Recycled Afterthought**

The work uses one sentence each from the other flash fictions with most being exactly as they were portrayed in the source material, subject to the persona's pronoun being changed to "you."

## About the Author and Artist

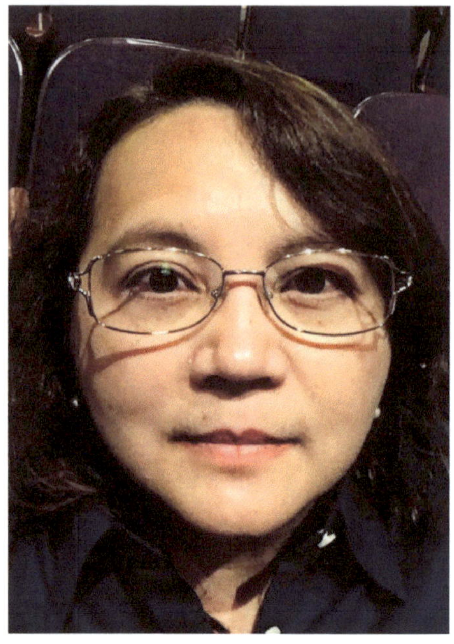

**Eileen R. Tabios** has released over 70 collections of poetry, fiction, essays, and experimental biographies from publishers in 10 countries and cyberspace. In 2023 she released the poetry collection *Because I Love You, I Become War*; an autobiography, *The Inventor;* and a flash fiction collection collaboration with harry k stammer, *Getting To One.* Other recent books include a first novel *DoveLion: A Fairy Tale for Our Times*; two French books, *PRISES (Double Take)* (trans. Fanny Garin) and *La Vie erotique de l'art* (trans. Samuel Rochery); and a book-length essay *Kapwa's Novels.* Her award-winning body of work includes invention of the hay(na)ku, a 21st century diasporic poetic form; the MDR Poetry Generator that can create poems totaling theoretical infinity; the "Flooid" poetry form that's rooted in a good deed; and a first poetry book, *Beyond Life Sentences*, which received the Philippines' National Book Award for Poetry. Translated into 12 languages, she also has edited, co-edited or conceptualized 15 anthologies of poetry, fiction and essays. Her writing and editing works have received recognition through awards, grants and residencies. More information is at http://eileenrtabios.com

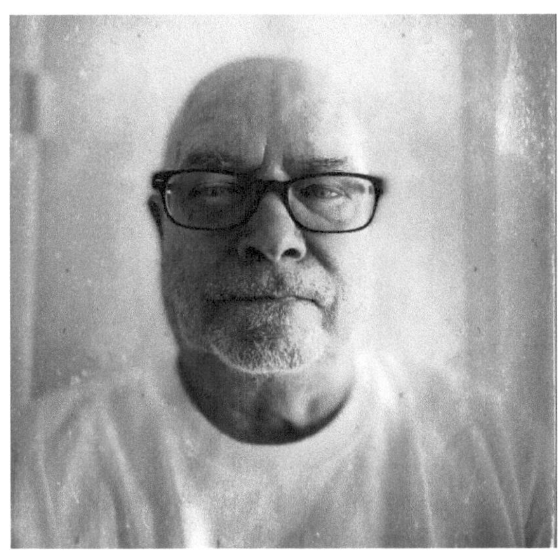

**harry k stammer** is a writer, musician and painter who lives and works in Santa Barbara, CA USA. His books include *every beyond't nothing* (persistencia), *tents* (Otoliths), *grounds* (Otoliths); and *tocsin* (Otoliths), *sidewalkss* (Concrete Mist Press), *walls't's* (Sandy Press) and *-48* (Sandy Press). Recent noise/poetry pieces are available at http://harrykstammer.bandcamp.com

www.ingramcontent.com/pod-product-compliance
Lightning Source LLC
LaVergne TN
LVHW052259100826
845147LV00001B/88

* 9 7 8 1 7 3 6 8 1 6 0 7 3 *